C000262399

A BOOT UP

GRASMERE & LANGDALE

Keith Wood

First published in Great Britain in 2010

British Library Cataloguing-in-Publication Data
A CIP record for this title is available from the British Library

ISBN 978 1 906887 79 7

PiXZ Books
Halsgrove House, Ryelands Industrial Estate,
Bagley Road, Wellington, Somerset TA21 9PZ
Tel: 01823 653777
Fax: 01823 216796
email: sales@halsgrove.com

An imprint of Halstar Ltd, part of the Halsgrove group of companies
Information on all Halsgrove titles is available at: www.halsgrove.com

Printed and bound in China by Toppan Leefung Printing Ltd

Contents

How to use this book

Langdale has long been known as a paradise for walkers and climbers and is as popular now as ever. Actually consisting of the twin valleys of Great and Little Langdale, it is to the head of Great Langdale that the eye is drawn with the iconic view of the Langdale Pikes. Whilst the Pikes may be the mountain celebrities their relatively modest height of around 2400 feet (725m) are dwarfed by their almost equally famous neighbours of Crinkle Crags and Bowfell at just under the magical 3000 feet mark (900m).

Just over the watershed to the north east lies the valley of Far Easedale with the picturesque Easedale Tarn and overlooked by the ridge from Calf Crag to Helm Crag, known to tourists as The Lion and the Lamb due its distinctive appearance from the main A591 running through the heart of the Lake District. Helm Crag descends into the village of Grasmere, probably best known as the home to the poet Wordsworth and his family, both Dove Cottage and Rydal Mount are open to visitors. Grasmere serves as the start point for three of the routes in this collection.

The majority of walks in this book are relatively easy to moderate and offer pleasant valley walking in this beautiful and varied landscape with ample opportunity to appreciate the surrounding high fells. For the more adventurous walks to the higher fells give a taste of true, mountain walking concluding with the classic walk over the Langdale Pikes from New Dungeon Ghyll visiting the high level Stickle Tarn overlooked by the massive cliffs of Pavey Ark. A total of five tarns are visited; Easedale Tarn, Blea Tarn, Red Tarn, Stickle Tarn and Little Langdale Tarn, together with the two lakes of Grasmere and Elterwater.

Each route is graded from Easy to More Challenging with details of distance, height ascended and the type of terrain covered, to help with decisions of which walk to choose.

All ten walks are covered by the

Ordnance Survey Explorer Maps OL6: The English Lakes, South-Western area, and OL7: The English Lakes, South-Eastern area, and Harvey's Lakeland Central Map. The maps in this book are only an outline version of each walk and the detail provided by the OS maps puts each route in context.

Every year tens of thousands of visitors enjoy the fells with the vast majority coming to no harm. However there are many cases each year where walkers are injured, get lost or find themselves in some other kind difficulty requiring the assistance of the Mountain Rescue Services. A few simple precautions should help avoid any problems:

- If you are unsure about your fitness start with the walks graded Easy and work your way up to More Challenging.
- Wear suitable footwear- properly fitted walking boots are recommended for all the walks.
- Take suitable clothing; the weather in the Lake District can change very quickly, take a waterproof and extra warm layers to wear.
- Take plenty to eat and drink en route, dehydration and lack of nourishment can lead to fatigue and mistakes being made.
- An outline map illustrates each walk but it is recommended that a complete map is taken.
- Inform someone of your planned route and expected return time.
- Check the weather forecast in advance and only take to the more challenging routes on clear days.
- And finally keep to the paths and watch where you are putting your feet – most accidents are caused by careless slips!

Useful websites:
Lake District National Park
www.lake-district.gov.uk
National Trust
www.nationaltrust.org.uk
Friends of the Lake District
www.fld.org.uk
Cumbria Tourism
www.golakes.co.uk
Lake District Outdoors
www.lakedistrictoutdoors.co.uk
Traveline – Public Transport Information
www.traveline.org.uk
Keith Wood Photography
www.keithwoodphotography.co.uk

Key to Symbols Used

Level of difficulty:

Easy 🌿

Fair 🌿 🌿

More challenging 🌿 🌿 🌿

Map symbols:

🚗   Park & start

–––––   Tarred Road

- - - - -   Footpath

■   Building / Town

+   Church

🍺   Pub

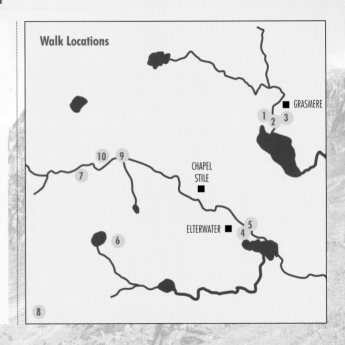

Walk Locations

GRASMERE

1 2 3

10 9

7

CHAPEL STILE

ELTERWATER   5 4

6

8

1 Easedale Tarn

Circuit of a famous high level tarn passing spectacular falls

Easedale Tarn is one of the most popular excursions undertaken from the village of Grasmere. The tarn which lies in a deep natural bowl at 925' high is overshadowed by the cliffs of Tarn Crag and Blea Rigg and serves as the source to one of the three Sour Milk Gills in the Lake District. This set of falls are passed on the way up to the tarn and were known as Churn Milk Force to Dorothy Wordsworth when she and her more famous poet bother William lived in Grasmere in the early nineteenth century.

Level: 🦋 🦋
Length: 5.75 miles (9.3km)
Ascent feet and m: 1100' (330m)
Terrain: Stony paths and some boggy ground
Park and Start: Red Bank Car Park, Grasmere (Grid ref 335 073)
Info: Public toilets and refreshments in Grasmere

Footbridge over Easedale Beck

1 Leave the Red Bank Road Car Park and head straight across the road around

Map labels: Easedale Gill, Easedale Tarn, Sour Milk Gill, Helm Crag, Waterfalls, Easedale, Blea Crag, Yew Crag, Grasmere, 1000 m

'New Bridge' over Easedale Beck

the back of the Dale Lodge Hotel. The road passes around the back of the village and the Grasmere Red Lion Hotel. Walk past the Heaton Cooper Studio and the village centre. Opposite Sam Reads Booksellers turn left to head up the Easedale Road signed; "Easedale Tarn". Walk along the road and at the earliest opportunity get off the road onto the Permissive path which runs parallel with the road. Back onto the road continue walking past Goody Bridge Farm.

(2) As the road swings around to the right take the footpath over the footbridge over Easedale Beck signposted to Easedale Tarn opposite a bright red wall mounted Post Box. Enter the National Trust's Easedale Estate and over a slate foot-bridge follow the path through the copse of trees and then through an iron gate. Follow the main track along the valley bottom with Easedale Beck on the right. The falls of Sour Milk Gill can already be seen crashing down the fellside ahead with the path just to its left. Helm Crag is in clear view to the right as you pass by the pack-horse bridge over Easedale Beck. Continue on the track with the beck still on the right. Through a gate and as the path crosses over a stream follow the "Public Bridleway" sign

Falls along Sour Milk Gill

straight on across the open pasture heading towards Sour Milk Gill. As the path passes through the drystone wall the path starts to gently on a well laid repaired pitched path up the hillside towards the falls. The path continues

to rise past the falls of Sour Milk Gill; a minor detour allows a closer inspection of the upper falls. Just past the falls the path levels off as it heads around the edge of a wide bowl with the beck now flowing through the middle. The return path can be seen on the other side of the beck. There is just one last climb beside the outflow of the tarn up to the tarn itself.

Pitched path up to Easedale Tarn

Next to Easedale Tarn is the site of a refreshment hut, one of several in the Lakes, popular with Victorian visitors. Light refreshments were available from the proprietor Mr Wilson, and many enjoyed boat trips out onto the Tarn. Gradually falling into disuse after WW2, the hut was demolished in the 1960s.

3 All of a sudden the magnificent spectacle of Easedale Tarn comes into view in its own natural bowl with Blea Crag and Tarn Crag overlooking this large high level tarn. Take a break at the tarn and the ruins of the old refreshment hut marked by a large solitary boulder and then choose whether to take a walk around the tarn or take the short cut across the stepping stones over the outflow to begin the return journey. To walk around the tarn continue on the main path along the left hand bank of the tarn with Tarn Crag towering above on the opposite bank. Veer off from the main path to pick up a narrow trod to go around the head of the tarn. Pick your place carefully across this wet ground. Cross over the stream which flows into the tarn and from here a clearer path around the head of the tarn emerges to take you around the other bank. Beneath Tarn Crag the path passes a ruined sheep fold.

Sour Milk Gill Falls

(4) Back at the outflow of the tarn the return route follows the opposite bank to the ascent. Continue on the clear path down to Easesdale with the beck now on the right hand side. Grasmere is in view in the valley bottom. The path enters the large bowl below the tarn and steadily descends. The path meanders around the edge of the bowl over well placed stepping stones to avoid wet feet. At the lip of the bowl the path veers away to the left, away from the beck, to start the descent into Far Easedale

with Helm Crag directly ahead. A short way down a huge heather topped boulder is marked with an arrow pointing the way to Grasmere. The path veers away from Grasmere into Easedale, follow the well placed yellow markers showing the way. The wooden footbridge crossing far Easedale Beck comes into view as you approach the valley bottom.

(5) Swing around to the right to join the path down Far Easedale along the valley bottom back towards Grasmere. Cross Far Easedale Gill over the wooden foot-bridge and continue heading down the valley following the route of Britain's favourite long distance trail the Coast to Coast. The route passes along the foot of Helm Crag. At the

back of some cottages a footpath sign clearly directs you towards Grasmere, through a gate and down a stone pitched enclosed lane. Shortly the

surfaced road is reached to take you all the way down into Grasmere and back to the start.

Easedale Tarn

2 Helm Crag & Far Easedale

A trip over Grasmere's favourite and distinctive fell top

Helm Crag is Grasmere's best known and best loved fell. What it lacks in height (a foot short of 1300') it more than makes up for in character with everyone that passes by on the busy and noisy A591 looking up to view the rocky crag known as "The Lion and the Lamb" on its summit ridge. With its clear paths and relatively low height Helm Crag makes a perfect outing for a half day, but in order to make a good day's outing this

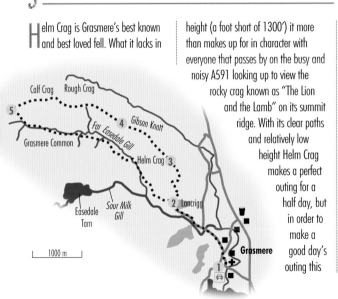

Level: 🐾 🐾 🐾
Length: 7.75 miles (12.4km)
Ascent feet and m: 2070' (630m)
Terrain: Stiff climb onto the ridge, undulating along the ridge and downhill all the way back
Park and Start: Red Bank Car Park, Grasmere (Grid ref 335 073)
Info: Public toilets and refreshments in Grasmere.

route continues along the fine ridge from Helm Crag, along to Gibson Knott and finally to Calf Crag – the highest point on the ridge at 1762' before making the return journey along the valley of Far Easedale.

13

1 Start from the Red Bank Car Park in the middle of Grasmere. Leave the Car Park and turn right to walk through Grasmere, heading towards the church. Turn left in front of the church and pass Sarah Nelson's Grasmere Gingerbread Shop. Pass the numerous hotels, outdoor shops and the Heaton Cooper Studio in front of the village green before turning left to go up the Easedale Road. Pass by the footbridge over the beck on the left and continue along the road. Helm Crag looms large to the front right. This walk along the road is a nice easy start before having to tackle the fairly steep ascent.

2 Pass through the hamlet towards the end off the road and arrive at a Y junction which is signed "Public Bridleway Easedale and Helm Crag". Take the right fork onto an un-surfaced lane starting to rise immediately. Pass through a wooden gate and continue on the track for barely 50 yards to arrive at another sign directing you up to the right marked Helm Crag. Walk up this ancient stony lane through the trees which opens out beneath Jackdaw

Grasmere from Helm Crag

All that remains is to follow the clear stony path straight up the front of Helm Crag. As height is gained look across to the left; Easedale Tarn comes into view. The rocky summit ridge is quickly reached; the first rocky outcrop is not the true summit but

In the 1850s Sarah Nelson took over the tenancy of 'Gate Cottage', originally the village school, next to the church in Grasmere. From there she made and sold Gingerbread to the passing Victorian tourists. The cottage remains largely unaltered and the smell of baking gingerbread, made to Sarah's secret recipe, still attracts the visitors.

Crag. Turn right to continue the ascent up the side of a long abandoned quarry. The well built path zig zags and rapidly gains height with views back down to Grasmere. The path continues ascending along the western flank of Helm Crag. A number of fine viewing stations of Easedale present themselves on this stage of the climb each giving a more than adequate excuse to stop and pause to regain ones breath. At a fairly substantial pile of stones – the path swings around to continue gently rising on grass slopes heading south. All of a sudden the ridge is crested bringing open views across the busy A591 below across to Fairfield and Seat Sandal.

what people driving north from Ambleside towards Keswick would recognise as "The Lion and the Lamb". The second more prominent crag along the ridge is the true summit and to my eyes clearly presents itself as "The Howitzer" from this angle but is also seen as "The Lion and the Lamb" when seen travelling south along the road. Take care along this part of the rocky ridge where there is plenty of potential for ankle twisting to arrive at the summit crag.

3 Now that hard work of the day is out of the way enjoy the walk along the ridge to Gibson Knott and Calf Crag. Walk past the Howitzer and initially descend, losing a couple of hundred feet which has to be immediately regained to head back

"The Howizter" summit of Helm Crag

up to Gibson Knott. There are outstanding views all the way along to the north along into Easedale where the return route along the valley can be clearly seen below. After another short climb the ridge line is regained

to reach the unimposing summit of Gibson Knott which marks the mid point of the ridge.

4 The path follows the ridge towards Calf Crag the highest point of the route at 1762'. It seems quite a long drag from Gibson Knott to Calf Crag including crossing some wet ground with peak hags the worst of which have had stones laid to ease the way across them. After about a mile the summit can be clearly seen ahead. A final climb and the rocky summit of Calf Crag is reached giving a fine view across Easedale to Deer Bields Crags opposite. It's down hill all the way from here, initially continuing to follow the ridge line heading towards a little scrap of water with Nab Crags in the foreground.

Summit of Gibson Knot

(5) Walk to the head of the valley to arrive at a junction of paths marked by a cairn and a couple of isolated rusty old fence posts. Take the left hand path where the path heading down Easedale starts by gently meandering downhill towards the foot of the valley for the long return. The young Far Easedale Gill is to the right falling in a series of mini cascades and further along a bigger fall joins from the left adjacent to a

Rowan tree. Cross over the beck by some well placed stepping stones which shouldn't present any difficulties even in spate. The two streams join together in a deep cleft to make a series of impressive falls. The path continues to lose height with the beck now cascading down on the left. A wooden footbridge lets you cross the widening Far Easedale Gill and to continue walking along the valley.

The path becomes an enclosed lane at a couple of stone barns and shortly arrives at the outbound junction. So now it's a matter of simply reversing your steps back into Grasmere. Now that you've burnt off some calories you deserve a treat and can call in for a slice or two of that delicious Sarah Nelson's Gingerbread on the way back to the car.

Easedale Tarn and Blea Rigg

Helm Crag & Far Easedale

Falls in Far Easedale

3 **Dow Bank above Grasmere**

A walk along the ridge separating Grasmere and Elterwater

St Oswald's
Kelbarrow

Silver
Howe

The
Wyke

Grasmere

Grasmere

Chapel Stile

Dow Bank

Red
Bank

1000 m

This is the third walk which starts from the main Red Bank Car Park in Grasmere but is the first to give us sight of the Langdale valley. Dow Bank is the name of the little ridge which separates Grasmere lake and Elterwater the guardian of Great Langdale. The walk itself is a joy giving great views down onto Grasmere on the ascent. Once the ridge is reached the view opens out to the west onto Elterwater and along Great Langdale. Whilst ideally suited to a sunday morning stroll or a summer's evening the walk is a delight at any time of the year.

Level: 🐾 🐾
Length: 3.5 miles (5.5km)
Ascent feet and m: 900′ (280m)
Terrain: Quiet roads and good clear paths
Park and Start: Red Bank Car Park, Grasmere (Grid ref 335 073)
Info: Public toilets and refreshments in Grasmere

Seat Sandal from Red Bank Road

Dow Bank above Grasmere

1 Park in the Red Bank Road Car Park in Grasmere. Turn left out of the Car Park to walk along the road heading towards Silver Howe passing the Goldril Hotel.

2 Opposite "Faeryland" tea rooms and just in front of Kelbarrow take the Public Footpath sign to the right through a gate up an enclosed unsurfaced lane. The lane rises gently up the hillside with views to the right towards Seat Sandal. Pass through the kissing gate at the top of the lane and follow the path up through the field beyond. Through another kissing gate at the top of the field and take the clear path heading towards Silver Howe with the intake wall on the left. As height is gradually gained views down onto Grasmere open up. Continue on the path gently rising up the fellside.

3 The path levels off at a cairn marking a junction of paths; right to Silver Howe, left to Grasmere but our route continues straight on, on the clear path through bracken heading towards the ridge of Dow Bank. Pass by some juniper bushes as a stream is crossed. The path continues to rise at this point with ever improving retrospective views of Grasmere and Rydal. Pass the remains of some long abandoned mining works.

4 The path flattens off as the ridge is reached at another crossroads of paths just past a large stone cairn. Turn left to walk along the humps and bumps of this super

Early on the ascent

little ridge offering great views into the adjoining valleys of Grasmere and Elterwater. From the raised land along the ridge you can look down into Langdale with Chapel Stile below with the bulk of Wetherlam and the great blott on the landscape of Hag Wood Slate Quarry to the west. Cross over a few stepping stones at the bottom of a wet saddle between the higher points along the ridge. Up a little rise to reach the highest point along the ridge of Dow Bank marked by a couple of well built cairns with great views all around including Crinckle Crags and Bowfell to the north at the head of Langdale. On the other side look down onto the twin lakes of Grasmere and Rydal Water with the village of Grasmere overlooked by the peaks of Helm Crag and Seat Sandal

First glimpse of Langdale

Dow Bank above Grasmere

Head of Great Langdale from the high point on Dow Bank

the National Trust's Nicholas Wood. Pass through another gate and continue to descend through the woods on a wide stony path. The path becomes a delightful enclosed lane.

Grasmere from Dow Bank

with the great mass of Fairfield to the east. Follow the path as it now falls quite steeply to eventually pass by a small sheet of water. The path descends seemingly heading towards Elterwater before meeting the main trans valley path from Elterwater over to Grasmere.

(5) Turn left onto the trans valley path and head towards a well built dry stone wall. The path heading back towards Grasmere is funnelled between two walls. Pass through the gate in the wall and continue with Grasmere back in view. Follow the clear path downhill into the trees of

6 Emerge onto a narrow surfaced road descending all the while. Continue on the occasionally busy Grasmere to Elterwater road all the way back to Grasmere

Tarn on Dow Bank

Dove Cottage, Grasmere, was the home of William Wordsworth from December 1799 to May 1808, where he produced his best work. Later the family moved to Rydal Mount. Wordsworth is buried in St Oswald's Churchyard, Grasmere, along with members of his family. Eight yew trees by the churchyard wall were planted by Wordsworth.

Seat Sandal and Grasmere from Red Bank Road

4 **Elterwater & Little Langdale**

A low level route passing by five of Lakeland's golden nuggets

Level: 🐾
Length: 5.5 miles (8.8km)
Ascent feet and m: 750′ (225m)
Terrain: Clear paths and lanes throughout
Park and Start: Elterwater National Trust Car Park (Grid ref 328 047)
Info: Refreshments from Britannia Inn, Elterwater

This gentle low level route through the centre of the Lake District is a real gem of a walk enabling the walker to enjoy five of 'Lakeland's golden nuggets'. The walk starts in the quiet village of Elterwater and starts by walking past the lake of the same name. The remainder of the walk follows the irregular route of the River Brathay, initially visiting Skelwith Force, where the river surges with immense power through a narrow cleft of rock, before continuing on at a gentler pace to Skelwith Bridge. Doubling back across Park How, the Brathay is rejoined just before arriving at the impressive Colwith Force, which is heard before it is seen. The route continues upstream before crossing the picturesque stone-built Slaters Bridge at the out-take of Little Langdale Tarn.

(map labels) Chapel Stile, Elterwater, Elterwater, Skelwith Bridge, Little Langdale, Little Fell, Park Fell, 1000 m, 2, 3, 4, 5, 6

1 Leave the National Trust Car Park through a small gate onto the well-laid path heading towards the lake by the side of Great Langdale Beck. Just before reaching the lake at a turn in the beck there are a couple of deep pools. The path turns away from the water and skirts around the edge of a small wooded area before veering back to continue along a good surfaced path along the edges of Elterwater through woodland. Leave the trees, proceed through the gate at the foot of the lake, where the view opens out across the reed beds at the edge of Elterwater up towards the Langdale Pikes.

2 Leaving the lake behind the path continues towards Skelwith Bridge through open fields

Langdale Pikes across Elterwater

following the banks of the river. At the end of the field pass through a five-bar gate into the woodland and follow the path through the trees.

3 The route continues by crossing over the new Woodburn Bridge (installed in November 2006) over

the river and follows the path of the Cumbria Way on slate chipping path through the woods. However before crossing the bridge continue for 100 yards to take a close look at Skelwith Falls crashing down the rocks before returning to the bridge. Keep to the main path through the woods around the back of Bridge House. As the path starts to rise at a T junction take the right hand path to continue walking up through the wood following the yellow waymarker sign for Cumbria Way and continue on the gently rising path up through the woods. Pass through a kissing gate to leave the woods and continue on the clear path. Where the path joins a farm lane, turn right following the waymarker. Pass Park House with fine views along Great Langdale and

Woodburn Bridge

oak woods keeping the riverbank to the right up to Colwith Force. After pausing to witness the impressive falls continue on your way. The route follows

Skelwith Force

follow the sign to Colwith. The route continues on through the fields, overlooking the the river down to the right. The path rises gently to the slate-built Park Farm, through the farmyard and continues following the

yellow waymarkers, eventually to reach a narrow road.

(4) Cross the road and climb the stile over the wall to pick up the path to Colwith. Walk through the

Apprentice piece at Park Farm

Garth. At the bottom of the hill cross over a packhorse bridge and continue following the lane as it loses its surface around a tree covered hillock. With a bridge and ford over the Brathay on your right, follow the sign to Hall Garth on an unsurfaced lane past the National Trust's Atkinson Coppice.

The lake of Elterwater, from the Old Norse meaning "lake of swans", is shortly passed. The lake is the smallest of the sixteen lakes and getting smaller each year as silt and other materials build up around its reed-fringed shoreline.

the riverbank through the trees and shortly the path climbs up through the trees. At the top of the woodland, leave the woods through a farmgate. Pass through a walled enclosure to reach High Park Farm through a kissing gate. Following the bridleway sign, go between the buildings and through a gate to join a narrow surfaced lane. Follow the lane to the right with Little Langdale to the front passing Stang End Farm with its vernacular barn. Continue down the lane signed to Tilberthwaite and Hall

(5) The picturesque Slaters Bridge appears over the wall to the right. Signed to Little Langdale, go through the gate, walk across the field to Slaters Bridge and over the Brathay. The path on the other side rises over a little knoll and Langdale Tarn is delightfully laid out beneath to the left. Pass through a kissing gate and field, two more farm gates and short lane before reaching the road beyond High Birk Howe farm.

(6) Turn left along the road and after 10 yards immediately turn right up another metalled lane. The lane passes Dale End Farm, where the surface breaks down past the farm. The track crosses open land above Fletcher's Wood heading across to Elterwater, before entering Sawrey's Wood. Continue on the lane down through the oak wood regaining views of Elterwater towards the bottom of the lane. At the bottom a track joins from the left and the lane now regains its surface. Pass Elterwater Hall and turn left onto the Elterwater to Colwith road to complete the journey back to the waiting car.

Colwith Woods

Slaters Bridge

5 Sawrey's Wood

A stroll through Sawrey's Wood and the village of Chapel Stile

This may be one of the shortest routes in this collection but it does take us on our first steps into Great Langdale. Once again starting from Elterwater the walk goes through the two centres of population in Langdale, namely the village of Elterwater itself and the nearby Chapel Stile. Inhabitants of both villages would have worked in the giant slate quarries around which this walk forms a circuit. Many of the buildings are constructed from the local slate including the church in Chapel Stile.

Path to join Cumbria Way and to Chapel Stile

Level:
Length: 2.75 miles (4.3km)
Ascent feet and m: 420' (125m)
Terrain: Clear paths and lanes throughout
Park and Start: Elterwater National Trust Car Park (Grid ref 328 047)
Info: Refreshments from Britannia Inn, Elterwater and Wainwright's Inn Chapel Stile

Bridge over Great Langdale Beck, Elterwater

① Park in the National Trust Car Park in Elterwater village just opposite the Britannia Inn. Leave the car park and turn left to walk along the road over the bridge over Great Langdale Beck. Pass Bridge End Cottage and follow the road for a few hundred yards passing the Elterwater YHA Youth Hostel. Just opposite Eltermere Old Barn the road forks; take the right hand road sign posted "Coniston Cycleway". Walk up the narrow surfaced lane past Elterwater Hall heading towards Sawrey's Wood.

② As the lane starts to lose its surface it forks again; take the lower right hand fork which is signed "No Through Road" walk along this lane heading into the trees. The walled lane gently rises up

Britannia Inn, Elterwater

through the wood and past the remains of slate quarry works. At the top of the rise pass by a cottage and continue straight on along the lane through the trees with glimpses of the still working quarry through the trees down to the right. Look out for

woodpeckers and maybe a glimpse of grey squirrels which have taken over this woodland. The lane starts to drop back down through the trees as it heads towards Baysbrown. As you leave the trees approaching Baysbrown the cliffs of Pavey Ark come into view on the horizon and Chapel Stile across the valley floor.

Scots pine near Baysbrown

(3) Just before the farm at Baysbrown take the sign "Path to Cumbria Way and Chapel Stile" to the right through a gate and

Sawrey's Wood

Bridge over Great Langdale Beck

and Elterwater. Follow the lane round to the left as it crosses the stone bridge over Great Langdale Beck. The lane swings around in front of a slate spoil heap heading to the village. As the lane heads towards the road keep straight on following the sign "Public

take this path around the farm buildings. Follow the wide unsurfaced track across the valley bottom through the busy summer campsite crossing over the stream called Baysbrown Pool.

(4) As the track approaches Great Langdale Beck at a T-junction of paths turn right to follow the Cumbria Way with the beck just on the left heading towards Chapel Stile

With hundreds of mineral mines and stone quarries, the Lake District became a centre for the manufacture of the explosives required. The Elterwater Gunpowder Works went into operation about 1824 and continued until the end of the First World War. The site of the works is now used for timeshare apartments.

Footpath to the Village Centre" along a narrow enclosed path with Chapel Stile just over the wall. Keep to path as it passes some buildings. As a road veers off to the left keep straight on around the back of Chapel Stile School following the waymarker and Footpath signs.

5 The path emerges onto the road opposite Langdale Village Hall and Brambles Café and Village Shop. Turn right along the road past Wainwright's Inn. Just past the inn take the Public Bridleway sign to the right to cross back over Great Langdale Beck over a footbridge. Over the bridge turn left again to pick up the path in front of the slate heap and to walk back. Leaving the slate behind the path rises for one last time through the trees and the path pops out onto the quarry road opposite a cavern. Turn left and walk back along the road to the start.

Chapel Stile

Great Langdale Beck

6 Lingmoor & Blea Tarn

A walk along the ridge overlooking Great Langdale

Standing between the twin valleys of Great Langdale and Little

Langdale; Lingmoor is ideally situated to give one of the best views in the whole of Lakeland at the fells around the head of Langdale. This short walk starts with a sharp climb to the top of Lingmoor before heading along the ridge with the head of Langdale in view all the way and concludes with a circuit of the delightful Blea Tarn with its own iconic view of the Langdale Pikes over the still waters of the tarn; save this one for a clear day!

Blake Rigg and Blea Tarn from the ascent

Level: 🐾 🐾
Length: 2.75 miles (4.4km)
Ascent feet and m: 1250' (380m)
Terrain: Steep pull to the top, followed by gentle descent on clear paths throughout
Park and Start: Blea Tarn National Trust Car Park (Grid ref 295 043)
Info: Refreshments: Old and New Dungeon Ghyll Hotels in Great Langdale

From the small National Trust Car Park next to Blea Tarn head back onto the road and turn left for barely 20 yards over a cattle grid and immediately head sharp left up the fellside with a wall immediately on the left and a stream trickling down on the right. This stiff pull rapidly gains height right from the start of the walk. After the steep start the rate of ascent slackens off as the path swings away from the wall towards

Blea Tarn from the ridge

the stream and crosses the first of two streams before heading up again on some loose rock. Cross over the second stream and again the path keeps relentlessly rising with the stream just to left. As height is gained Crinkle Crags and Bowfell come into sight over Blea Tarn. A much clearer path appears as the plateau of Birk Knott is reached. Approaching the ridge line the path re-crosses the top of the stream and again follows closely the line of the wall. The path drops down an annoying depression past a stand of wind blasted trees before continuing straight up the wall for the last 80m or 250' or so to gain the summit. All of a sudden the wire fence which runs along the spine of the fell comes into view with the main summit cairn of Brown How. The highest point of the ridge is just the other side of the fence, cross over the stile to take in the panoramic views.

Side Pike and Langdale Pikes from the depression

(2) The way forward proceeds to the north-west along a clear path adjacent to the ruined wall and wire fence which follows the crest of the ridge gradually losing height heading towards Side Pike. There are great view in the foreground all the way along, Blea Tarn comes into view down on the left whilst Lingmoor Tarn is just down to the right. Keep straight on along the ridge as the wall takes a turn to descend the fellside. The path goes over a rocky knoll before continuing its descent to Side Pike with both Old and New Dungeon Ghyll Hotels in view at the foot of the Langdale Pikes. Approaching a series of stone walls

the path descends quite steeply to arrive at a stile crossing the line of the wall; the path continues following the ridgeline towards Side Pike but now with the main wall on the right.

3 At the depression between Side Pike and Lingmoor a wire fence is reached; turn left, do not cross the fence, head down the fell-side on the clear path with the wire fence on the right. There is a good view of Blea Tarn as the path steeply descends down to the road below. Just before the road there is a wooden stile over the wire fence, cross over and continue on the path which runs around the lower flanks of Side Pike to avoid walking along the narrow road. Approaching the top of the pass, follow the path through a gap in the wall

Side Pike

Bridge over Bleamoss Beck

5 All that remains is to cross the wooden footbridge over the outflow of the tarn; Bleamoss Beck and follow the wide path across the foot of the tarn back to the start with that iconic view of the Langdale Pikes overlooking Blea Tarn.

In the late summer the fells of Cumbria become a swathe of purple. Bell heather, ling (Lingmoor's name originates from the Old Norse word lyng meaning "heather covered") and cross-leaved heath are dominant, but amongst them can also be found bilberry, crowberry, cowberry and the rare bearberry.

and drop down to the road through the gate or over the ladder stile.

4 Cross the road and head to the pair of gates though the wall onto the wide track which heads down to walk down around the back of Blea Tarn. This wide loose surfaced track is the easiest walking of the route on the level to the tarn and offers a good view to the left of the ridge along the top of Lingmoor. The reed beds at the end of the tarn are soon passed and the path enters the coniferous wood which borders the west side of the tarn its worthwhile to make a short detour onto the spur jutting into to the tarn before continuing on to the end.

Langdale Pikes over Blea Tarn

7 Mickleden

A gentle stroll along Mickleden with high mountains on either side

The valley of Mickleden serves as an extension of the main Great Langdale valley even deeper into the heart of the high mountains. Overlooked by the twin peaks of Loft Crag and Pike O' Stickle to the north and by the great rising ridge of The Band leading to Bowfell to the south. Guarding the head of the valley to the west is Rossett Pike with Rossett Gill and Stake Gill to either side. This short walk starting from the Old Dungeon Ghyll Hotel, the birthplace of rock climbing in Langdale, goes half way down the valley giving plenty of opportunity to appreciate the surrounding mountains.

Level:
Length: 2.3 miles (3.7km)
Ascent feet and m: Negligible
Terrain: Easy walking along clear paths along the valley bottom
Park and Start: National Trust Old Dungeon Ghyll Car Park
Info: Refreshments: Old Dungeon Ghyll Hotel

Start of Mickleden

Start from the National Trust Old Dungeon Ghyll Car Park. Leave the Car Park and walk around the back of the hotel on the surfaced lane. As the road swings up to the right keep walking straight on following the Path sign onto the stony path with a gate at the end and Bowfell straight ahead. Pass through the gate and walk straight on along the path just above the wall heading towards Mickleden. With Raven Crag immediately above on the right pass by Middle Fell Farm below on the left. This popular path, another stretch of the Cumbria Way, heads into the heart of the mountains at the head of Great Langdale with Pike o' Blisco to the left, Crinkle Crags ahead and the mass of Bowfell to the front right with the fields in the valley bottom below.

Middle Fell Farm with Pike of Blisco in the distance

As the path proceeds deeper into Mickleden the distinctive shape of Pike o' Stickle appears above to the right and Rossett Pike appears on the horizon at the head of the valley with Stool End Farm at the end of The Band in the valley bottom on the left. The path swings around to the right to go beneath Pike o' Stickle heading straight down the valley with the deep cleft of Rossett Gill in sight at the head of the valley.

For over three hundred years, Old Dungeon Ghyll, originally a farm and inn, has offered accommodation and food to weary travellers. A popular meeting place for walkers, cyclists and famous mountaineers, the property was the first in Langdale to be owned by the National Trust. It is named after nearby Dungeon Ghyll Force

2 As the valley opens out and the end of the wall on the left is reached simply cross the grass heading towards Mickleden Beck. Cross over the beck using either the footbridge or ford to reach the clear path on the opposite bank. Having reached the bank turn left and walk

along the clear path heading back along the valley with The Band up to the right. Join a farmer's track as it rounds the end of a drystone wall and walk along the track as it passes through a walled enclosure. Follow the footpath with its slate sign

around to the right and after barely 50 yards swing back around to the left and through a gate with a drystone wall now on the left as the route heads to Stool End Farm. Pike o' Stickle and Loft Crag, two of the Langdale Pikes, are on the left and

Crinkle Crags and The Band

Rossett Pike at the head of the valley

looking down the valley Side Pike and Lingmoor are now in the foreground. The rough stony path heads along beside the wall to reach Stool End Farm past a copse of mixed woodland.

(3) The path goes around the back of the farm buildings. Follow the sign on a gate through the farmyard and then the clear signs through the farm buildings around to the right and back around the sheep pens onto the surfaced lane to head back to Old Dungeon Ghyll Hotel. Walk back along the surfaced road along the valley bottom over a cattle grid. The road crosses over Oxendale Beck. As you reach the road, turn immediately to the left following the sign "Public Way" to the Old Dungeon Ghyll Car Park. With the hotel and Car Park in sight cross over the Packhorse Bridge, follow the footpath signs back to the start.

Langdale Pikes

8 Pike of Blisco

A short stiff climb to a stunning viewing station

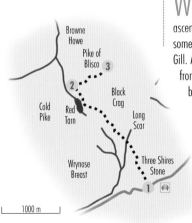

Browne Howe
Pike of Blisco 3
2
Black Crag
Cold Pike
Red Tarn
Long Scar
Wrynose Breast
Three Shires Stone 1
1000 m

Whilst Pike o' Blisco belongs to Langdale the main route of ascent from Great Langdale involves some 2000 feet of ascent up Browney Gill. Alternatively this back door route from the summit of Wrynose Pass between Little Langdale and Dunnerdale gives the advantage of some 1000 feet already gained in the car. This is not only an easy way to climb Pike o' Blisco itself but also to get into the heart of the mountains which surround the head of

Level: 🐾 🐾 🐾
Length: 2.75 miles (4.5km)
Ascent feet and m: 1125' (340m)
Terrain: Typical Lakeland high level paths, stiff climb to the summit
Park and Start: Roadside parking at top of Wrynose Pass (Grid ref 276 026)
Info: No facilities on route

Great Langdale with intimate views of Crinkle Crags and Bowfell. A marvellous short journey which delivers views far beyond the effort required both of high mountains and from the summit of Pike o' Blisco itself full length views of both Great and Little Langdale valleys.

Three Shires Stone

① Start from the top of Wrynose Pass next to the Three Shires Stone where there is limited off road parking. A finger post; "Public Footpath" points the way into the hills up towards Red Tarn. Leaving the road from the top of the pass the gravel and stony path makes its way to the north. After a short distance the view opens out to the left down Wrynose Pass to Cockley Beck with Harter Fell filling the view at the end of the valley. After crossing a hillside stream the popular path starts to gently rise up the fellside. Route finding is very easy — just keep following the clear and popular path which continues rising. Cross over another mountain stream where the lower crags of Pike o' Blisco appear to the front right, but the summit lies hidden beyond. In addition to giving a rapid and easy route to the top of Pike o' Blisco and its twin Cold Pike the path is popular for being an easy route to one of the icons of the Lake District namely Crinckle Crags. The stony path meanders along the flanks of Pike o' Blisco and glimpses of Crinckle Crags start to be seen to the front left. As the path levels off approaching Red Tarn the path becomes wet in places underfoot

Great Knott and Crinckle Crags

especially following periods of heavy rain. Before long the secluded mountain tarn of Red Tarn comes into view overlooked by Cold Pike and the view opens out to reveal the dramatic vista of Great Knott, the Crinckles and the ridge of Bowfell in the distance. The path continues passing by Red Tarn and the path turns red underfoot as iron ore is near the surface.

(2) Upon reaching a T junction of paths turn right for the short but steep climb up the path to the

summit of Pike o' Blisco. This clear but rough and rocky path rises up the fellside leaving Red Tarn far below. Don't be ashamed to pause for breath on this sharp climb; there are ample excuses to stop and admire the ever improving views. It's an unremittingly steep climb to the top.

(3) The top is reached and the view unfolds giving a panoramic view including sight of most of the other walks within the collection including a full length view along Great Langdale and Little Langdale separated by Lingmoor. The Langdale Pikes with the Helvellyn range in the distance are to the east, Windermere and Coniston Water to the south continuing to look around to the Coniston Fells of Wetherlam and

Red Tarn and Cold Pike

Swirl How and then round to the west with Crinckle Crags and Bowfell. Take your time to enjoy the magnificent views from the impressive stone-built

cairn which marks the summit at 2304 feet (705m). All that remains is to carefully retrace your steps back down to the tarn and then the out-

Langdale Pikes from Pike of Blisco

The Wrynose Pass is a narrow, winding road that climbs to 393m (1281 feet) and is one of the steepest roads in Cumbria. At its summit the Three Shire Stone is a boundary stone which marks the location at which the historic counties of Lancashire, Cumberland and Westmorland met.

bound path back to the top of Wrynose Pass. What seemed an unremitting climb turns into a relatively easy descent back to the tarn. Heading back to the road at Wrynose Pass the impressive bulk of Wetherlam and the pointed summit of Swirl How are in view most of the way back to the start.

Great Knott, Crinckle Crags and Bowfell from the slopes of Pike of Blisco

9 Great Langdale Valley

A gentle stroll along the valley bottom in the heart of Great Langdale

This is a great little walk to enjoy on a quiet day off from the fells. A gentle stroll along the floor of the valley whilst others are toiling up the high fells. Great Langdale is a walker's paradise and this short walk along either side of Great Langdale Beck showcases the high fells all around to great effect. As a photographer the temptation is always to aim for the high ground for the best views, but all too frequently the best scenes are those from the valley floor looking up to the high fells and this walk serves to aptly prove the point.

Level:

Length: 2.75 miles (4.3km)

Ascent feet and m: 250' (75m)

Terrain: Easy walking on clear paths and a disused road

Park and Start: National Trust Stickle Ghyll Car Park (Grid ref 294 063)

Info: Refreshments Stickle Barn Tavern and the New Dungeon Ghyll Hotel

"This way at the start"

Public Footpath
← Oak Howe
1 mile

1000 m

Park in the National Trust Stickle Ghyll Car Park adjacent to the New Dungeon Ghyll Hotel. Leave the Car Park and immediately cross the road and go through a gate onto a farmer's track across the valley bottom signposted "Public Footpath Oak Howe 1 mile". The track crosses the field and over a stone bridge across Great Langdale Beck. Crinkle Crags and Bowfell are to the right at the head of the valley. Continue on the farm track with Side Pike directly in front as you approach Side House Farm.

The path swings around to the left to pass in front of Side House. Follow both the metal footpath sign and yellow waymarker through a kissing gate and over a wooden footbridge to walk along the valley bottom following the route of the Cumbria Way Long Distance Trail. Through another kissing gate and the path starts to gently rise up the fellside on a well laid pitched stone path along the flanks of Lingmoor. As the path levels out to head along the side of Lingmoor pause to look back over your shoulder towards the head

Fellside above Dungeon Ghyll

In the 1800s smugglers used the Langdale valley routes to bring alcohol from the Isle of Man, on pack-horses from the coast. The Langdales were also the home of the famous moonshiner Lanty Slee, who even supplied his illicit wares to the local magistrate – this did not stop him spending much time in the local gaol.

of the valley and the Langdale Pikes. The path passes through a sheepfold before crossing over the beck coming down from Lingmoor Tarn. The path now heads along the lower slopes of Lingmoor on a well used stony path. After a while the path drops down to meet the intake wall and gently

descends towards the valley floor with Great Langdale Beck on the left flowing between its restraining walls which are there to prevent flooding. Pass through a gate in a wall and continue along the path which rises again. Follow the yellow

waymarker as the path enters a narrow walled lane. Notice the large boulder in the field to the right fallen from the Oakhowe Crags above. The lane turns sharply to the right and continues along the valley bottom.

Bridge over Great Langdale Beck

Side House Farm

farm track through the fields up to the road. Approaching the road the lane is enclosed by a slate wall.

4 Pass through a kissing gate to emerge onto the road, turn left and walk along the road for barely 50 yards where, just before a red Post Box, a lane heads off to the left away from the road signed "Public Byway to Dungeon Ghyll". This lane, the Old

Langdale Pikes

3 At the T junction of paths at Oak Howe follow the sign straight on along the "Public Bridleway to Great Langdale Road 1/3 mile". Pass a barn and Oak How Cottage where the track swings around to the left towards the middle of the valley. Approaching a footbridge over the beck leave the main track and cross over the bridge. Follow the Public Bridleway to Langdale Road now just ¼ mile away along the wide

Langdale Road, heads back to the middle of the valley and swings round to the right to follow along the valley floor heading back to Dungeon Ghyll. The iconic view of the Langdale Pikes fills the view ahead all the way along. As you approach New Dungeon Ghyll the fells around the head of the valley fill the view ahead. Approaching the Dungeon Ghyll the lane follows the course of the river, walk through the LDNP Car Park and back onto the road where the start is barely another 50 yards along.

Pass through the sheepfold

Traditional Post Box at start of the Old Langdale Road

10 The Langdale Pikes

A true fell walk over the iconic Langdale Pikes

Level: 🥾 🥾 🥾
Length: 5 miles (7.5km)
Ascent feet and m: 2500' (750m)
Terrain: A full blown fell walk on clear paths with some steep sections of both ascent and descent
Park and Start: LDNP Car Park at New Dungeon Ghyll Hotel (Grid ref 295 063)
Info: Refreshments from New Dungeon Ghyll Hotel and Stickle Barn Tavern

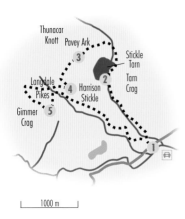

The Langdale Pikes are one of the renowned views in the Lake District; from a distance the classic outline appears to consist of just two peaks, in truth the Pikes consist of four separate summits. These being from left to right of the iconic view the shapely Pike of Stickle, Loft Crag, Harrison Stickle (the highest of the group at 2403' or 736m) and Pavey Ark; the massive cliffs which tower above Stickle Tarn. For the walk itself we're going to reverse the listing starting with the climb up to Stickle Tarn and Pavey Ark to eventually finish

on Loft Crag. If you're one of those walkers who need warming up before getting on with a climb, this walk won't be for you, as almost immediately from leaving the car hard climbing begins.

Pike Howe and Harrison Stickle on the ascent

1 Start from the Lake District National Park Car Park in Greater Langdale just opposite the New Dungeon Ghyll Hotel. Walk up the lane towards the hotel following the Public Bridleway sign to New Dungeon Ghyll. Pass the hotel on the right and the whitewashed Stickle Cottage. Take the Public Bridleway to the right of Stickle Cottage, pass through the gate and the intake wall, to walk through an enclosure and over a wooden footbridge over a beck. The climbing begins immediately beside Stickle Ghyll and after about 50 yards cross over a slate bridge and follow the footpath sign to Whitegill Crag. You're already ascending quite quickly on the repaired path beside Stickle Ghyll with Harrison Stickle ahead and Pike Howe to the left.

Harrison Stickle across Stickle Tarn

After passing through a gap in a wall cross back over the beck and just keep plodding on upwards with the ghyll on your left all the while. Stickle Ghyll Falls are passed as you keep steadily rising. The rate of ascent eases for a while as a bowl opens out just below Tarn Crag at the top of Stickle Ghyll Falls. Keep on rising and after a little scramble cross over

High above the valley in Langdale, on the scree slopes of Pike O' Stickle, is the famous stone age axe factory were thousands of stone axe heads were produced. Axes from Langdale have been found in places as far apart as Northern Ireland and Peterborough.

Stickle Ghyll one last time using the massive boulders, for the last pull up to Stickle Tarn. After one final boulder strewn climb the great cliff face of Pavey Ark gradually reveals itself to finally open out with Harrison Stickle to the left and Pavey Ark to the front above Stickle Tarn, a great place to stop for a well earned breather to enjoy the surroundings.

(2) Cross the outflow of the tarn and walk right, around Stickle Tarn beneath Pavey Ark. Cross the inflow and then take the path beside Bright Beck off to the left. After a couple of hundred yards the path forks, take the left hand fork to cross over the beck and take the clear and stony path heading up the side of Pavey Ark known as North Rake which

Looking down onto Pavey Ark and Stickle Tarn from Harrison Stickle

around to Harrison Stickle. Eventually a path of sorts materialises which swings around making its way to Harrison Stickle. You need to keep your wits about you to watch where you're placing your feet through this boulder field to avoid twisted ankles. After a final little scramble the rocky summit of Harrison Stickle is reached and an extraordinary panoramic view as befits this central location in the Lake District opens out.

heads steeply upwards. At a minor plateau marked by a huge cairn the view opens out to the south with a spectacular view looking down onto Stickle Tarn, before resuming the rocky boulder strewn ascent. The path flattens out as the plateau behind

Pavey Ark is reached; fork off to the left on one of the myriad of little tracks to reach the summit looking down onto Stickle Tarn.

 To continue, pick your way through the rocks, heading

 Having had your fill of the view it's easy enough to bag the two remaining Pikes; Pike o' Stickle and Loft Crag. There are a couple of paths leading off the back of Harrison Stickle, it doesn't matter which one you take as both lead to the boggy col at the top of Dungeon

Great Langdale from Harrison Stickle

Ghyll. Cross the marsh between Harrison Stickle and Pike o' Stickle over the boulders on the prepared path, pick up the clear path heading up to Pike o' Stickle where there is a final scramble to make the summit pinnacle. Clamber back down and take the clear path along the ridge to Loft Crag, enjoying the view from Loft Crag looking down into Mickleden.

5 From Loft Crag make your way back down to the marsh and join the main path on the left hand bank of Dungeon Ghyll for the relatively short but steep descent all the way back down to the valley bottom. At the top of the ghyll the cliffs of Harrison Stickle tower above and rushing water can be heard below in the bottom of the ravine as the

path starts to descend. The rocky knoll of Pike Howe acts a constant guide to the front with full length views along Langdale. As height is lost the path veers away from the ghyll. Just before reaching Pike Howe the path veers around the right of the knoll, but it's well worth the extra little bit of effort to clamber onto the top of Pike Howe for one last view along Langdale. Resuming the descent the path swings around to the right of Pike Howe and continues to drop steeply down with the ghyll deep down on the right. Cross a stile through the intake wall and nearing the valley bottom pass through a gate in the corner of two walls to join with the footpath from Mickleden. Finally pass through a kissing gate and follow the path down to the back of the hotel.

Pike Howe and Great Langdale from the descent